Less Mess

Less Stress

**Minimalist Routines to Declutter Your
Environment,
Unload Your Mind and Optimize Your Day**

Gain Control Over Your Life

By **Zoe McKey**

Communication Coach and

Social Development Trainer

zoemckey@gmail.com
www.zoemckey.com

Thank you for choosing my book! I would like to show my appreciation for the trust you gave me by giving a **FREE GIFT** for you!

Visit: www.zoemckey.com to get it!

The checklist talks about *5 key elements of building self-confidence* and contains extra actionable worksheets with practice exercises for deeper learning.

Learn how to:

- Solve 80% of you self-esteem issues with one simple change
- Keep your confidence permanent without falling back to self-doubt
- Not fall into the trap of promising words
- Overcome anxiety
- Be confident among other people

TABLE OF CONTENTS

Introduction

I used to wonder what the hype around minimalism was about. What is minimalism anyway? I understood the word, I could construct a vague picture around this noun, but I could hardly grasp what I was supposed to do with it.

Google is our friend, so first I searched for answers there. But as you may know, it's Google's nature to give a lot of explanations and my results returned fifteen different explanations just on the first page. And does anyone ever click on page two? Right? It is kind of an unwritten rule of minimalist Google users to never click on page two — there's nothing worthwhile there.

Everything that matters is on page one, and if it is not, it doesn't exist.

In any case, I didn't give up my quest to understand the nature of minimalism, and I started digging deeper. I turned to Google's arch-nemesis – YouTube. I found the same chaotic results – hacks, Ted talks, white walls, Japanese men living with two pairs of socks, Pinterest...

I really wanted to understand the myth of minimalism. I needed it. Last year, I was about to move home, finally stepping out from the rat race of university life, two jobs, and an unfulfilled life filled with things. But for some reason, the information was so random and disconnected that I had a hard time finding what I needed.

But I needed to simplify stuff. Not just my things, but also my relationships, and my way of thinking. And getting worked up about finding the right definitions and habits of minimalism was not a good start. So, I took a deep breath, and let go of my perfectionist desire for knowledge. I didn't want to do these things by the book. I wanted to find my own answers.

I had four months to simplify my life in a way that would grant me an easy transition from working a full-time job and being a student and lonely warrior to becoming a self-employed writer and world-traveler who shares her life with someone.

Living alone for ten years made me too stiff, too independent in spirit, but too dependent on the things I collected to keep me company. Being alone, I got too attached to every friendship — regardless of how they affected my life.

At least she or he cares about me, spends time with me, opens up about her or his miserable life and complaints. This is a sign of trust, isn't it? This was how I rationalized those cluttered connections I had. I bet many of us do.

Of course, I came to the realization that soon all this would be over. I would leave this place, leave these people and everything that had all the meaning in the world. From then on, my previous life would be only a gradually fading fragment of memory. And I was tight on time. So, I had none to waste.

I wanted to do a thorough job with my decluttering, so first I made an inventory of everything I had: 10 forks, 10... oops, 9 spoons (I must have left one at my previous flat... damn it!), 11 knives. Wait what? Why? From where...

I had two Jeep-loads full of stuff, so I don't want to enter in every detail. For three months I took inventory — three notebooks full of my stuff, numbers and what not. I felt like the world's stupidest person, and like I was making the biggest decisions of my life. For example, how many small pillowcases will I need? Or, should I or shouldn't I, throw away that half-used hair conditioner? But duh... It's still half-full. (In these cases it's never half-empty.)

The clock was ticking. I sat with my ocean of stuff plus three notebooks filled with my inventory. I hadn't even been thinking about minimalism in the past three months. I felt I was on a mission, all my things deserved this much attention, they'd served me faithfully. Even those things that I never used. They stuck with me, and kept me company.

Like that super-sharp knife from Top Shop that I never used for cooking, but was handy when I suspected a burglar was in my house. I still remember how ferociously I jumped into the kitchen waving it when I heard a puffing noise at 3 am. It turned out I'd left the kitchen window open and the wind was blowing across the top of the empty Pringles can I hadn't throw out for weeks because I wanted to store rice in it!!!

This was me: the ultimate hoarder. I tell these half-funny and half-pitiful stories to let you know how far I was from being a minimalist. I had many things, many acquaintances, and many small, time-filling hobbies that I felt too guilty to stop doing.

So, one day, when I felt I'd never be able to step out of my mental block, I went to my balcony where, weirdly enough, I only had one chair and a broom. My dad called it the "landing station for tired witches." So, I sat at my landing station on a beautiful April afternoon, and I watched the neighbor's two cherry trees bloom in front of my eyes. They were gorgeous. And I felt like the most tired witch. So, I just watched and watched those trees.

The more I watched, the more a thought squirmed into my head. Both cherry trees were beautiful, but they were both different. One of them was tall, fully blooming, thick with flowers, and smelled – just stunning! The other was smaller, thinner with fewer flowers, but somehow flourishing in a... *minimalist beauty.*

In that moment, I understood what minimalism was – to me at least. It is not a numbers game, as many people think. It is not about having less or more, but about being intentional about whatever you let into your life. *Minimalism is the mindset that helps you realize what has value in your life now, and what will be important later. Once you know, you can let go of what doesn't serve you anymore.*

Those two cherry trees were both perfect: the full one and the sparser one too. If minimalism was a thing for cherry trees, the dense one would feel pretty overwhelmed. But it isn't – its flowers are perfect and equally important. However, when the time comes, the cherry tree lets go of its flowers to make space for the next step, knowing that it will have flowers again when it needs them.

That is a roundabout way to explain what I discovered that day, so here's a less abstract version. I knew my things were valuable and some even had a sentimental value, but I also understood that in my new life they would not be useful anymore. It was time to let them go and give them to someone who really needed them. This was how I felt about the people I left behind too.

Let me repeat my definition of minimalism: it is the mindset that helps you realize what has value in your life now and in the future so you can let go of what doesn't. This doesn't apply only to physical items, it applies to all the areas of your life: habits, beliefs, relationships, health, work, etc.

Minimalism is not about more or less, therefore you can't be "minimalist enough." It is, rather, a mental crutch that helps you realize what has value in your life. The more values you discover, the easier it becomes to appreciate what you have. Add the feeling of gratitude for what you have and for what you're about to let go of and be happy. That's the ultimate goal of minimalism.

After those two cherry trees outsmarted Google and YouTube, my decluttering mission took a 180-degree turn, and I successfully finished everything I needed to in the last month. Not only did I get rid of 75 percent of my stuff, I figured out all my useless relationships, past offenses, and let go of fears and inner mental blocks that resisted my lifestyle change and so on. But, I found an evergreen method to help me live my life in a more simple, free, and happy way even long after moving.

This book is about how you can benefit from my last month's journey through the many realms of minimalism. How you can use the power of minimalism to simplify all the areas of your life, how you can maintain a minimalist attitude even after you've decluttered your life, and how to feel happy and free as a result.

Chapter 1: "Start With Why"

I'm sorry to disappoint you, but this chapter's title has nothing to do with Simon Sinek's book, *Start With Why* except for the main idea his book is built around: starting with why instead of what and how. It is an incredibly inspiring creation, so if you want to take the idea of "start with why" to the next level, my chapter title is a hint of where to start.

When it comes to minimalism, it is important to search your brain and soul and ask why you are interested in simplifying those particular areas of your life.

What are the feelings that lead you to cast your vote for simplicity instead of complexity? Some people consider something that is complex more advanced, better, more difficult, or smarter, right? What is the powerful miracle in simple things then? Are simplicity and minimalism the same thing?

To answer this question let's dig deeper into the history of minimalism. Originally, the word minimalism was used to describe a style of design or art. Starting in the 60s and 70s, in America, as a derived aspect of modernism, minimalism was the new pared-down trend in music, filmography, poetry, and interior design. It was also a countered response to abstract expressionism, the other art trend of the post-World War II era.

Nowadays, when we mention minimalism, we are more often describing a person who lives with a minimal number of things. The champion of owning little is Andrew Hyde, a backpacker who began traveling around the world in 2010. He is the proud owner of no more than 39 items (mostly clothes and electronic devices). If you want to read a list of these 39 items, check out the following link:

http://andrewhy.de/minimalism-project-update-39-things/. I find it to be impressive.

And this is how minimalism is mainly interpreted today. People owning only 100 things, a tiny flat where not even two hairbreadths can cross each other. No clutter, nothing.

There are others who use the word minimalism for living simply. Sometimes I get the impression that people think owning less and living simply are interchangeable concepts. I think there's a difference between the two.

And this is why it is so important to start with the "why" before jumping into the world of minimalism. What is your purpose? Is it to only declutter your home? Or are you seeking a lifestyle change that includes having more stuff, and you really are looking for more of a mental state makeover? Do you feel overwhelmed by your multitude of thoughts, obligations, hobbies, or the people in your life?

Whatever your purpose is, you're not wrong. I believe minimalism today has many interpretations. Since you started reading this book you might have started to think about what it means to you?

It is possible that none of the definitions or options I told you or that you read about minimalism correspond to what it means to you. In some definitions, you find this concept represents a high-standard idea of simplicity that is impossible to live up to. But here's the good news about minimalism being such a broad concept, since there is no clear answer to the question of what minimalism is, you can define it for yourself.

To be honest, when I first heard about minimalism my first thought was that it was strictly about decluttering, living with one pair of socks in a white studio with white walls, furniture, and books covered in white A4 sheets of paper. If this is how you define it, amazing. There's nothing wrong with it, but this description doesn't exhaust the concept.

After the cherry tree experience, I understood that minimalism is not a numbers game. I don't have to throw away all of my things until I am left with only 100 to be a minimalist. I repeat, if you want to do all these things, great, but you don't have to.

What is the easiest way to define your "whys?"

1. Analyze your brain-flow. Why did you choose minimalism?

Is it because you want to declutter your environment? Why do you think your environment is cluttered? Is it full of things you don't use, is it because of stuff that reminds you of bad memories or an ended relationship? Or do you simply want to re-decorate your flat in a way that allows you to breathe easier?

Is it because you generally want to live a simpler lifestyle? Does this imply establishing a less-crowded and less-stressful life rather than getting rid of things per se? Does it mean having fewer obligations, commitments to people, and less pressure from the consumer society to buy buy

buy? Does it mean more free time in nature with your loved ones and so on?

Or, through minimalism do you seek a better internal balance? Less damaging thoughts? To let go of ideas that clearly make you feel miserable and pull you back?

Fewer social expectations and dress codes? Less pressure to live up to family demands? etc.

Is it because minimalism is trendy and being a minimalist will make you feel cooler? Why is coolness important to you? Or anything else you associate with minimalism?

2. When you have your "why," set your goals.

Like every habit, lifestyle, or belief change, becoming a minimalist also takes time. It is a long-term commitment. On one hand because only doing it persistently will make the results stick, on the other hand, because if you do it too fast, invest too much energy in it at the beginning, you will lose sight of the initial concept: being simple.

If you push it to the limits – cleaning your two-story house in two days, throwing out everything – you'll be sick of it by the time you finish. You'll think something like, *phew, I'm done with this minimalism crap for a decade, I don't want to hear any more about it. Where's that Target flier?* And yes, you resume right where you left off.

The wonderful thing about minimalism is that there's no stress involved. I've never heard of a company threatening its employees that if they didn't adapt to minimalism they'll get fired. Or a husband saying, "I can't live with you anymore because you don't serve my dinners minimalist enough!!"

Approaching life with a minimalist mindset is a change you do for yourself because you want it. Therefore, there is no other pressure on you than the one you conceive for yourself. It is up to you how quickly you want to get rid of stuff, or select people to remove from your life, or whatever your goal may be. And if minimalism is not a number's game, it's certainly not an "in time" game.

When you have your goals, just chill and start doing whatever you had in mind. Since there shouldn't be any external pressure, becoming more minimalist is your wish, it shouldn't be too hard to follow your desire.

In a nutshell, this is the structure of "start with why." You may wonder, that's it? How should I set these goals? This is too vague. Don't worry. I'm just about to answer these questions as I promised in the chapter before. Now that I've written this parenthesis chapter about the decision-making process (which is a very important cornerstone, this makes your minimalist mindset permanent instead of a quick fire) let's go more in-depth into the main life areas where you can use minimalism.

I won't discuss the original meaning of minimalism – when it is an art or design – I leave that to the artists. If you're seeking that, you won't find much information about it in this book. But even so, stick with me, the self-help minimalist, and see how colorful that black and white rainbow is.

Chapter 2: Minimalism As Life-Changing Magic

Have you read the famous book by Marie Kondo, *The Life-Changing Magic of Tiding Up*? I did. And it was indeed life-changing. I remember sitting on my tired witch landing station with a coffee in one hand and my Kindle in the other. It was the day after the cherry tree enlightenment.

Before I continue this thread, let me insert a footnote here. As I mentioned in the previous two chapters, you can interpret minimalism as you wish and apply only actions you feel you need. However, I constructed this book to be an external and internal, shallow and in-depth, life-changing and casual, complete minimalism makeover guide for those who want to see the connections and domino effect minimalist mindset can have on all aspects of human life. If you don't want to convert into a humming minimalist (with a normal, happy life – I must add) that's totally cool. In this case, just start your commitment in the one or two areas you wish to minimalize. Ok, footnote ended.

So, I sat on the balcony, coffee, Kindle, Marie Kondo. I had a special case, right: I needed to move my things back home after ten years so I could start my traveling career. Since one can't deny genetics, you can guess my parents were a more advanced version of hoarders than I.

My dad, an engineer and political hustler, is the uncrowned king of hoarding in the family. Yogurt cups, plastic bags, VHS player manuals, shoe boxes, food boxes, big boxes, small boxes, cardboard boxes, wooden boxes, new boxes, broken boxes…

"You can never know when they will come in handy! When the Russians will invade again and we'll be forced to run away. We'll need the boxes then…" Yes, like that is a real possibility, but even IF someone does invade us, my dad needs the boxes for the rest of the trash he and my grandparents have accumulated. We keep their stuff at home too, since we sold their house after they died. Our house is not too small nor is it too big. It's not a size that can accept the dandy fortune of three generations. Still, this is the place where I have to make my own trash fit.

Help me, Marie Kondo, help me!

Ok, I chased away these horrible visions of my sad future and started reading the book. I was very curious to learn what this pocket-size book knew so well that it stayed on the top shelf of the New York Times best-seller list for so long. I wanted a new life. Since I'd quit my job, left my university, started my writer career, and moved (mostly my stuff) home, and myself to the USA for the short period of time a tourist visa permits, I was really dedicated to doing this thing right.

Let me share you some highlights from that book:

Marie Kondo believes tiding up is a special event, not an endless, everyday chore. It is a big, one-time selection. Tidying is not about dusting the house and folding everything because soon clutter will invade your house again. She says that a person has to experience only once the ultimate state of cleanliness in order to be able to maintain it.

And how to go about the process of tiding up? Kondo says that it is better to sort things by category, not by room. She told a story of her high school years when she went home and started cleaning out her drawers. She sorted out the toothbrushes, the makeup samples, and others by category and left them in the same drawers. The next day she opened another drawer and, surprise, she found the same cluttered items she'd found the day before. She realized that we tend to store the same type of items, sometimes owning multiple of them, in different areas. If we clean a room and arrange everything, we won't necessarily get rid of useless or duplicate items.

If we want to translate this into minimalisms language it would sound something like: do not own two items that serve the same purpose. When you want to get rid of clutter, the best way to do it is to go through your rooms and make selections by category.

Here's how I did it. I had a relatively big kitchen. That was the courtroom. I put four big bed sheets on the floor. On one bed sheet, I poured all my clothing; on the second I put healthcare products (makeup, hair stuff, cleaning stuff, vitamins... everything that fit under that umbrella); on the third, I sorted all my kitchen equipment; and on the fourth I put everything else, the black box, the gate to Mordor, and the items I needed the least.

There was one especially good point in Marie Kondo's book, so as point three, let me dispense it: she said *respect your belongings*. I took a look at all my sad stuff lying on the ground, crying for utility. I knew I wouldn't use most of it because I had one of them already, or because my parents had one, and there was no chance they'd throw out the silver spoons of generations.

I wouldn't like my beloved things to end up in the trash either. But it is not good to be constantly jammed, kicked, or propped at the bottom of the wardrobe, just because I can't find the inner strength to say goodbye to them. It is even disrespectful for me to just kick them into the corner. It is better to give them to someone who really needs them instead of intoxicating my environment and awakening a feeling of guilt in my heart for not using them. But still, you know, sometimes it is difficult to say goodbye to your childhood treasures or a gift your late grandfather gave you.

So, as I sat there, filled with nostalgia (a very bad advisor when it comes to de-cluttering according to M. Kondo) a thought invaded my mind – I am so lucky to own all these things. Minimalism is not only a concept but a measure of luck. I chose to get rid of my possessions intentionally to live with just the necessary amount of stuff. I could literally see the role good fortune and privilege plays in that.

Being able to create an environment you love is a privilege, decluttering is a privilege. Being able to decide what has value in your life, letting go when something doesn't – doesn't that make you feel lucky and privileged? To be able to afford that in your life? If you don't like the clothes in your closet, you can go to the mall and buy other things. You don't have to stick to items you don't use anymore just for the sake of thinking *it might be handy in... 25 years*. No. If you'll need it again, you'll be able to get it then. That's true privilege.

The more I thought about how to declutter for the sake of a more mobile, balanced life, the surer I became of something: things don't have any purpose if they don't make you happy in some way. Just as I read in *The Life-Changing Magic of Tiding Up*. If I look at an item and I don't feel a spark of joy, that item would be in better care with somebody else.

And let's keep it real, people – you won't feel a spark of joy looking at your toothbrush, but it's a necessity. One toothbrush. This rule applies to every necessity. Or even if it is a necessary item, but you have five of them. What value do the other four add to your life? Is it so important to have five sharp knives? Oh, the fifth is only for holidays? Will the turkey get offended and dry itself because you cut it with the regular knife?

My grandmother, may she rest in peace, did these things. She had a different dinner set and silverware so as not to shame herself with the ones we used every day when guests came around. She even had a "clean room" which was like zone 404 for me as a kid. This secret chamber only opened up when someone came to visit. Old world upbringing. I still struggle to understand why she kept a separate house-worth of stuff for guests. It didn't make her happy, that's for sure.

She constantly complained about how big the house was, how many things were in there, and how difficult it was for her to be in charge of all of it.

For a millennial, this kind of lifestyle sounds almost unimaginable. It is hard to grasp the other side – when people are needy.

Think about those people who only buy what they value, because that's the only thing they can afford. And yes, there are people who can't even do that.

When there are so many people who don't have enough to begin with, how can I sit here throwing myself a pity party for my first-world problem – only having one month left to simplify my life?

Maybe you think, *true, there are many poor people, but why should I get depressed thinking about what they lack?* You shouldn't. Don't feel bad because you are lucky and privileged to have extra things that they don't. It is also true that you can't help everyone, but you can help somebody with some of your valueless valuables. For that person, it may be invaluable.

Don't forget to practice gratitude for what you have, because your life is about to get even better by decluttering the things you can. You know your circumstances may change, nothing lasts forever, and how lucky it is that the day of change is not today. (It may never come, don't worry. Just be prepared.)

So, here's how I got rid of my physical things and embraced the spirit of minimalism and the advice I read in Marie Kondo's bestselling book.

As I mentioned before, I separated my things onto the four separate sheets. I organized them into categories. I started with my clothing. Since I was about to start a nomadic life, I knew I had to be merciless on this one. If you face different circumstances and you just want to minimalize your closet for the sake of a style change, you don't have to do it in such an extreme way.

Start by throwing out those clothes that are unwearable. The thousand-year-old pajamas and the nice shirt with the huge coffee stain have to go. You wouldn't wear these and wouldn't give them away either. If you are sentimental, say goodbye to them. Be especially severe with underwear. You know what I mean. I think this is the easiest way to start getting rid of things (be it clothing or something else): start with the stuff that must go in the trash.

When you're done with the trash, select the clothes you wear most often and without which you couldn't imagine the sun rising in the east. To not fall into excess, keep yourself to the magic of the number 3. Choose your top 3 shirts, top 3 trousers, jackets, shoes, etc. Again, this can apply to your other categories too. For example, you'd never want to be parted from your super expensive non-stick pan, the similarly expensive (non-holiday) knife, and electric kitchen scale. Take these out from the courtroom. They're innocent and not too much.

When you've sorted out the trash and the must-keeps, then comes the challenging part. The rest. This stuff is not your everyday wear, but it is still wearable. You just need to lose ten pounds, or buy a new muffin-baking sheet for it. (You burned the little bastards in the previous one so badly that you couldn't scratch the remains out. Oh, did I say you? I meant me.) These things are the hardest to select.

Here comes the spark of joy into this picture. Take each individual piece and if you feel that you love that thing and you'd use it in the next month, keep it. If you feel attached, but you're not sure you'd use it in the next month, leave it with the rest of the things for now. This might take some time. You don't have to do it all on one day.

Whenever you're done, put the *I will use these this month* items next to the *must keep* items.

Then go through the remaining things again, and put those you felt attached to and that you think you might use in the next six months into a cardboard box (if you don't have any, email me, we have plenty) and take these boxes to a storage space you that is separate from your living space.

You can even hire a company to store these things for you for a certain amount of money. Even better, when we pay for something, we value it much more – and it is also a pain in the ass if we spend that money for nothing.

If, in that half-a-year period, you take out anything from those boxes to use them, cool. Keep that particular thing. But for the rest of the things lying in the garage or in some storage unit – they have to go. You didn't need them, you probably lived just fine without them and IF, MAYBE, PERHAPS, one day you'll need something from there, trust that you'll be able to buy it again.

And the final category: those things that are not trash, but you know you won't use in the next six months or more (ever maybe). Put them into a box and find the best place to donate them. I, for example, used Facebook to find a place to donate my things. I contacted a Hungarian goodwill group, and in half an hour I found a family who needed the clothes, a village school for my school supplies, and a homeless shelter for my kitchen equipment and bedroom things (quilts, pillows, what not).

I don't mean to show off by saying this. But, I can truly tell you that those moments when I brought my things to their new owners were some of the happiest moments of my life. The faces of those people filled my heart with so much joy and fulfillment that I started weeping when we said goodbye. This is what I call a truly win-win situation.

This is how I got rid of most of my personal belongings in less than a month. And it wasn't exhausting at all. Each day I spent a maximum of 30 minutes doing the decluttering process I explained above. Finding the trashy ones, the must-keep ones, and packing the leftovers to give to someone else are easy steps. The selection of the one to six month pieces is more difficult. But this is a special event as Marie Kondo calls it, not an everyday event. So, chill, take the time you need to make the best decisions. Don't procrastinate, but don't stress yourself out either. I had a deadline – either I would get rid of my stuff or my landlord would do it.

And no. Don't throw out your Christmas tree ornaments just because you wouldn't use them in the next six months. Minimalism is not a numbers game – Maybe I should make a shirt with this phrase on it. The point here is to reduce the number of belongings necessary for your comfort, needs, and desires. You want this. So clearly, there's no point in throwing out something that you'd use the next day.

That's the basic rule: keep one of everything that is necessary for you to operate your everyday life without being needy. If you're the mother of three this will be more, if you're a backpacker this will be less.

Aiming for a more decluttered environment is just one way you can simplify your life. In the following chapters, I'll talk about other areas of life where you can apply a minimalist mindset. I share the lessons I learned embracing this lifestyle, changing my mindset, figuring out what matters most to me – be it physical belongings or more abstract concepts such as friendship, love, or happiness. I present universal thoughts through an individual's experiences; therefore, I accept that I may not be the right voice to you. But I'm still a voice and you might find it to be the echo of yours. If I can help you with my voice, I've fulfilled my mission. If I can't, I hope you'll find what you're looking for.

Chapter 3: A Beautiful, Minimalist Mind

Minimalism as a mindset doesn't mean that you'll get rid of 25,000 of your 50,000 daily thoughts. It's more about switching off the thing I call the mixer of the brain. You know, it's like when you want to bake something, and you have five random ingredients at home. You know in the beginning that if you start baking with those five, nothing good would come of it.

The same applies to our thoughts. Sometimes we want to find a solution, a best option among those few thoughts we currently have in our minds. We throw it all in: loud neighbor, better self-worth,

45

need for a pet, high taxes, daddy issues. This all goes into the mixer of the brain. Shake them together and there you go, the perfect recipe for anxiety and mental clutter. We know we shouldn't mix them like that, but it just happens.

Like it or not, this is what our brain does. It blows my mind that the human nervous system has been evolving for more than 600 years, and it still hasn't gotten over its ancient negativity wiring. I have the feeling that I have put this in all of my books, so why leave it out of this one – the story of our grand grand grand... fathers and mothers living hundreds of thousands of years ago, and expecting the worst all the time. And yes, this expectation assured their survival. It also helped make you able to worry about your mental clutter and minimalism breakthrough today.

But talking seriously about this subject, overcomplicating our thoughts that our brain has an oversupply of anyway, can cause great deterioration in our quality of life. And if you are devoted to changing your life to the better and simpler, like I did, you should consider committing not only to physical decluttering but also mental.

One of the best books I've read on this topic is *Declutter Your Mind* by Steve Scott and Barrie Davenport. The book is pretty complex, not only about mental decluttering, but also about relationships, life-obligations, and surroundings.

I read this book after my own personal mental decluttering so I will refer only to those parts of the book that were present in my personal journey – like the causes of mental clutter, for instance.

You probably won't drop your jaw in shock when I say that one of the most common causes of being mentally overwhelmed is stress. This is why I emphasize not to stress about your new minimalist routines. When you add your "legitimate worries and concerns," as Steve and Barrie phrase it, to your generated stressors, it adds up to make you less focused, anxious, tired, and unhappy.

The mind also faces decision fatigue at each corner. I observed this best when I went to the US. So many options, so many things to buy — clothes, food, electronics. Sales here and sales there. I couldn't go to the grocery without spending at least half an hour examining all my options and a million types of rosemary condiments. Which is cheaper? Which is more expensive but a better value? By the time I left the store with the best rosemary to fit my needs, my brain was exhausted.

But you don't have to go to the store for decision fatigue to strike. It can happen in your own kitchen too. Five sharp knives? Which one will cut the chicken breast best? Environmental clutter has a great effect on your mental overload. So somehow these different fields of life where you can use a minimalist mindset, are interconnected. I exhausted the question of how to get rid of your extra stuff in the previous chapter.

And yet I didn't mention the mental clutter our human relationships can cause. Did she reply yet? No?? Why??? And an ocean-full of thoughts invade your mind to seek the reason why this is happening. Even if deep down you know the only person who has an answer for that is the girl in question. You can't think with someone else's brain.

Sometimes you feel your brain is so exhausted and overloaded that when someone asks you a question later you feel like you didn't give the right answer. Or, that you could have given a better answer. You start stressing and wondering if that person now considers you a simple-minded fool. You see, the interpersonal thought thread is dancing a wild dance again. Now I'll stop giving examples of how twisted our brain is. I don't want to give any more disturbing "aha" moments.

Before I get started with how to declutter your mind, analyze your thoughts. What are they telling you now? What's your biggest mental tangle? Stress? Decision fatigue? Negative thoughts? Interpersonal interactions?

How can you simplify all this? I believe that mental minimalism (shall I call it M&M?) isn't a numbers game either. It's not about having fewer thoughts a day, ignoring emotions or cutting off the consumerist tangle we face. That's impossible. In fact, if we try too hard to stop something or cut something off, it complicates our thoughts too much.

You know the game "don't think about the pink elephant" don't you? In case you don't, it's just a mind game: somebody randomly tells you to not think about a pink elephant or you lose. What's your very first thought? Right? The same applies to stressors or negative thoughts: don't think about it (or you'll attract it). What should I not think about? Aha, the traffic jam, aha, the limiting beliefs, aha, stress. And there you go; you're thinking about them already.

The key to mental minimalism is acceptance, introspection, and selfishness. This seems a bit odd. That's it Zoe? That's your great advice? To be selfish? Really?!

Let me explain.

Why acceptance?

Today, I think the fighter attitude is more valued than the more compromising or accepting ones. The former is considered to be brave, and the latter is considered to be a coward. Whereas, most of our mental clutter comes from the fighter attitude.

Don't get me wrong. I'm not saying you shouldn't defend yourself when you face a real injustice. But, let's admit it, we fight perceived or irrelevant injustices more often, and we stay silent for the real ones. If we stay silent in front of real injustice, we feel like cowards. "Oh, I didn't have the guts to tell Tom that he was wrong about me." Or, "I accepted the mistreatment of my partner to keep the peace, but I feel bad about it." Since the world admires the fighter attitude, we want to compensate for it somewhere else – in the supermarket, in traffic, or with employees. These are low-risk territories.

But this is a double-edged sword. We get mental clutter from two sides. We feel frustrated about not fighting when it was right, and about fighting when it's not necessary, so we get stressed for nothing. (I'd like to clarify, that having a fighter attitude doesn't mean picking a verbal or physical fight. It's a way of imposing self-respect in hostile circumstances.)

But there are so many times when it's not worth having a fighter attitude. In fact, except in those cases when a real injustice strikes us (or we are in a competition), we shouldn't use it.

It simplifies our thoughts enormously if we accept some inalienable truths. If we accept that there will be a traffic jam at 5 o'clock and that our journey will be longer, we approach the day with a totally different spirit. Since we accepted it is not a stress anymore, we plan accordingly. Download a new audiobook or some groovy music. Or, we can take the risk of leaving earlier or later than 5 o'clock, but we should accept that there's no guarantee there won't be traffic then either. Sure, you can let your inner fighter loose and you can press the horn like a champion, but what's the point?

The same rule applies to shopping. You can keep your mind busy with prices, quality, and the big variety. Think about it, sulk about it, write a pamphlet about it on Facebook, but at the end of the day, it won't change. Or you can just accept that (even if you'd have been better off in the 18th century) we live in the 21st century now. It's capitalism and everybody wants to earn their money.

It's not a global conspiracy against you and me to sell five types of rosemary condiments. They don't keep me there on purpose; I'm the one who is hesitant to choose between the cheaper and the better value. The moment I understood this, I became much more chill about grocery shopping. I intended to finish it as soon as possible, but I also accepted that it might take up to 30 minutes based on my decisions. I can always value my time more and pick the first one, or value my money, and take the time to make the best choice.

It's not the world, it's me.

Mental minimalism is taking responsibility for what you can control, and accepting what you cannot. Life becomes incredibly simple this way.

Every stress or anxiety can be broken-down to either something you can control but tossed to someone else, or to something you wanted to control but could not (therefore you didn't accept it).

I could invent exercises, tell you to write down this or that, but there isn't anything to write about this. You have to be in the moment, have to be mindful so that when the moment comes you can remind yourself, *oh, I can control this. If I take the risk it is my responsibility.* If you really want a writing exercise, maybe this will be the most useful:

Think about and write down your biggest stressors that cause the most mental entanglement. Break them down to major characteristics. Find a prevention tool.

For example, if you know you hate traffic, standing in line, or listening to someone else's stupidity, I'll break-down your diagnosis: you're impatient. How to handle impatience is the topic of many books, but not this one. This is about simplifying, and thus improving your mental processing. You need to find a prevention tool to help you with unavoidable situations that trigger impatience. For example, always keep a book at hand. You can have it in Kindle form on your phone. No excuses. Every time your mind starts to wander, start reading the book.

Did you know if you read just 15 minutes a day, you'll be able to finish 35-40 medium length books a year?

You can write a small reminder note and put it somewhere you're likely to notice it often. Like make your phone's screensaver your favorite funny character with the keywords responsibility + control, acceptance + uncontrollable. And thus, when you start checking time on your phone when you're super annoyed you'll see it and remember.

Why introspection?

What do I mean by this? Many people seek validation or answers to their problems from external sources. These sources will provide answers. They can be answers of their best knowledge or just of the leave-me-alone, I-don't-care type. Whatever their answer might be, it's not a sure thing that it will resonate with your internal belief system. You'll struggle to accept it, but somehow there will always be a weird unease that will manifest itself in lots of whys and hows — totally unnecessary mental clutter.

Why introspection? To simplify the road to your heart and give yourself peace of mind. When you have a question, try to find your own answers to them first. If you are unhappy with your answer or want perspective, hear out someone else.

The worst mental clutter is from the internal conflicts and regrets you have about what you've spent your days, weeks, years (life) believing because someone else said you should. Acceptance is difficult when you realize at the age of 55 that you didn't want to be a lawyer, but you did only because your parents insisted you should embrace this profession for more money.

Seek inside your mind what are the questions you want to answer, and, when you find your answer, really admit it. Don't start making it nicer sounding, or more fitting to the social norms. It's just you and your head. Don't feel ashamed of who you are.

Some things you can't change about yourself. Some you can. What should you do with both? Hmm? That's right: accept what you can't change and take responsibility to change what you can.

Introspection is a form of meditation. In many books, including *Declutter Your Mind*, I read about meditation as a solution for mental decluttering.

I'll tell you what I did do in that last month before moving and changing my life, I walked to work. It was a good 10 km walk, therefore it took me about 1.5 hours to arrive at work. Since I could make most of my journey on the Danube riverbank, most of this walk showcased the world-class beauty of Budapest —sunset, springtime, beautiful, pleasant breezes, nice chatter, and light music from the boats.

I was intentional with my introspection. I chose to walk there to think through everything I wanted before I left. Closing ten years of resentments, pain, issues, and saying goodbye to similar amounts of happy moments, wasn't easy. Two funny facts about this 1.5-hour walk: before I started doing it, I lived with the constant conviction that I never had enough time. *No time, no time, I'm busy, no time, gonna rush, ok?* As soon as I decided that I wanted this 1.5 hours for myself, somehow, magically, a time-space continuum opened up and I found the time.

How? It's about being intentional. It makes a huge difference when you wake up with the thought that you're busy so not sure you'll be able to do what you do. Or if you wake up with the thought that you'll walk the 1.5 hours even though you're busy. Somehow your mind programs itself to that event. Less Facebook, better decision making during the day, I don't know how, but it happens.

The other funny fact: the first day I did my mental minimalism makeover walk I didn't know that it will take 1.5 hours. I got an estimate on Google Maps for it, but I wasn't sure. I didn't try it. So, 90 percent of my mental attention centered on my fear of being late. I imagined ten ways I'd be late, ten scoldings from my boss, and made up ten excuses. I rushed through that first walk. I was huffing and puffing, not enjoying the river, or sunset, thinking *shut up music, can't you see I try to be introspective here?!* I arrived at my workplace in one hour and twenty-five minutes. Since I had left home early, my arrival was too early. I was tired, sweaty, with the nerves frayed.

The next day, I decided to trust that I'd arrive on time. I also accepted that something might come up or deter me so I wouldn't make it on time, but by then I'd had the experience of what I could do on the journey in 80 minutes. So, I let my mind fly, thinking about my happiest and saddest moments in that city. What did I learn? How did I grow from that mistake I made four years ago? I watched the beautiful scenery, letting the noises and smells in. I felt blessed to walk in the sunset in one of the most beautiful cities in the world. I stopped to watch a street performer. I gave guidance to tourists... I felt relaxed. My mind was jumping on a tambourine of a thousand thoughts, still I felt relaxed mentally. And, I arrived at work in one hour and twenty-six minutes.

That day I learned an important lesson. All that stress, those negative thoughts, that huffing and puffing, the insensitivity to the surroundings, and fear were adding up to save me six minutes. I won six minutes, pleased my boss by being early, but I lost everything else – which would have been for me. And this leads to my last point of mental minimalism.

Why selfishness?

I feel that people give being selfish a bad name. And sure, if it extends to an extreme, it's unhealthy. But so is selflessness – at an extreme it is spiritual suicide.

Like it or not, we humans are selfish. Maybe there are some Buddhist priests who are not, but since that's not you, don't make that the norm. That's the exception, and unless you want to become a Buddhist priest yourself, don't take that as your reality. It isn't and it will bring you inner conflict.

Sometimes I feel that I say things that are quite contrary to what the common message is. And that's ok. The more different voices you hear in this space, the better. I could define this best by using Derek Siver's thoughts.

"I'm just the counter-melody. I may love the melody too, but I don't want to just duplicate it. So, I try to think of a good counter-melody. I do it to compensate for something I think is missing in the common message."

My counter-melody is promoting selfishness as being the third pillar of mental minimalism. Isn't life much easier if you first ask yourself:

> Do I like this or not?
> Do I approve this or not?
> Am I happy or not?

And if the answer is yes, then start philosophizing about what impact your decision has on others.

But we tend to make it the other way around. When it comes to making a decision first you carefully take into consideration the interest of everyone else: children, spouse, family, friends, colleagues, the lady at the corner shop, your dogs… You make your decision based on this hierarchy and if it overlaps with your needs, then you're lucky. But usually, like 99 percent of the time, you aren't.

And this is when "what ifs" and "maybes" invade your mind like the plague. You feel anxious, but you won't speak up in an effort to not disturb others' peace of mind.

Now you might think, *ok, so I should be like a bulldozer? Me, me, me while I make others' lives miserable?* Certainly not. But are these really the only two options? What I recommend here is making the decision for yourself first and then starting the process of compromising with the other party. There are so many *force majeure* life events you don't choose and you can't control like illnesses, catastrophes, and others. Take responsibility to control those you can: like your life as an individual.

If you start living your life asking yourself "hell yeah?" or "nope" first, everything will be much easier. This is what I mean by being selfish. Be selfish enough to take the burden of inner conflicts and what ifs off your shoulders. Do not be insensitive with others' feelings, but or your own. That's it.

These three things together - acceptance, introspection, and selfishness - will help make decisions much easier. Your life will become less complicated and you'll face much fewer annoying factors around you.

If you are really committed to your desire to simplify your mental overload, you'll find these three steps easy to make, not because they are easy to execute – it is a challenge to accept seemingly unfair or disturbing events, but who will suffer the most if they are not accepted? That's right, you. So being eager to accept situations, being willing to take the time to introspect, and being a bit selfish sometimes will make you happier.

Sometimes I wonder which comes first: happiness or simplicity. Being more flexible, self-aware, and self-directed makes you happy first, and when you're happy everything seems simple. Or maybe these three steps take a lot decision fatigue off your shoulders therefore you feel happy. Maybe, depending on the situation, both orders can be right.

Long story short, making these three changes in your daily cognitive routines will make your life easier and you happier. They cost you nothing and they are not complicated at all. So, what do you have to lose? Give them a try.

Chapter 4: Reducing or Redirecting Redundant Relationships

This chapter title must be a grueling riddle for Japanese people or those who can't pronounce the letter "r." I used to have trouble saying "RubbeR" too, when I was a kid. My grandmother grew tired of teaching me pronouncing the letter "r" properly. But sometimes, when I talk too quickly I tend to miss the correct pronunciation of "r." And there is a difference between rush and lush, isn't there?

Anyway, my point here wasn't to make fun of myself or other people who struggle with the letter "r," but to introduce the story of when I first felt that some people simply didn't have a place in my life, and that I shouldn't persuade myself otherwise.

As you may know with children, everything that is imperfect, or stands out is a potential target. And so were my speaking skills in pre-school.

Some of them became my friends just to listen to me and collect all the words I mispronounced in order to compose a poem which they posted on my drawer to shame me one Tuesday morning. For some reason, my threat, "you'll leglet it!!!" wasn't very effective. Still a mystery why.

I felt humiliated, hurt, and treated unfairly. And when I stood alone, ostracized, a little boy came to talk to me. I was convinced he was mute until then because he never spoke with anyone:

"Don't wolly, I underlstand youl feelings. My mommy said it can be collected and one day I'll be able to plonounce lettel L light. So will you."

It's alright for you to laugh now, but I wasn't laughing that day. I was almost crying. I connected with this little boy and I felt understood, I found my place in the r-less world. I wanted to please all the cool kids, I never felt truly accepted, but I didn't let my hopes die that one day they would. This anxious desire to comply made me insecure and fragile in those few months while it lasted.

But thanks to the little boy, I could see quickly, even as a kid what a difference it can make to have a few likeminded people around. You can have them for free, or you sell your soul to the devil trying to please many others who are different. I was best-friends with this boy in my childhood. We still keep in touch. He still can't pronounce "r" but, let me tell you, he has charmed more girls than any of his friends. How? By making fun of his mispronunciation. He uses words with the most "rs" and makes girls laugh a lot. He's brilliant. He should teach it. He didn't give up, he accepted that he's like this and worked to turn his weakness into his strength.

He's the best example I know of the saying "forge your weakness into strength and it will become your toughest shield, which annihilates every arrow."

But I feel I got carried away with my story – I can when I unleash my brain into the field of memories. So back to our topic: minimalism in relationships.

By this point, I'm pretty sure you know what I'm about to say: minimalism is not a numbers game. This applies to human relationships, too. It's not about how many or few friends you have, but about how much trouble and mental fatigue they cause.

To make this equation simple: those people who build you up and charge after you when you see them are making your life happier, and therefore easier (because everything seems easier when you're happy). And those who use your conversations to pour out a tub of problems, and to complain to you and bring you down make your mind more exhausted, negative, and even catastrophizing. (*My friend is right; the end of the world is near!! How lucky he reminded me, I almost forgot.*)

Based on what we learned in the previous chapter, these people often trigger our fight mentality. We can start seeing threats even where there's nothing there. Not to mention that sorrowful atmosphere can drain physical and mental energy. Do you remember your last big fight, when you struggled and then cried heavily? Do you recall how utterly tired you felt afterward? Did your brain feel empty, even slightly dizzy, and your body powerless? This is what a massive negative experience does to you.

Now recall your most recent joyful conversation: a promotion, a proposal, or even just a stimulating exchange of ideas. Did you felt like your mind was buzzing, fully charged? Did your body feel ready to challenge Shakira to a hip shaking dance? This is what a massive positive experience does for you.

You need people who you love in your life because even though they may sometimes drive you nuts and can be the cause of a lot of mental clutter, they are also the reason for your fundamental happiness. But the ratio of good to bad memories matters. If someone makes you sad and depressed almost all the time, it's time for you to evaluate how much you're willing to sacrifice your happiness to maintain that relationship, and how much harder your life becomes with them in it.

What about family? We have a saying in Hungary that you can't choose your relatives, only your friends. But you can certainly choose who you spend more time with. The good news is that even though you can't choose your relatives, you can choose how much time and effort you spend with them. It's a tough situation if your mom, dad, or siblings drag you down. Still, at the end of the day, you have to choose to be loyal to them or yourself. You are responsible for your own happiness and so are they. If you feel dragged down by them, it's your responsibility to take action.

And no, it won't be easy. You'll be the selfish one who only cares about herself. But, who does somebody who calls you selfish want you to care about? That's right, them. So, who's the selfish one?

This is why you shouldn't be concerned if someone is upset by your retreat from the relationship or friendship. The person who wants to keep you in it even though he or she knows that connection doesn't help you, is not a real friend. People who really care about you accept you unconditionally. Therefore, they also accept the fact that you want some distance.

Of course, if a relative or friend makes you upset, it's only fair to give them a warning before you decide to withdraw from the friendship. Tell your friend what bothers you, try to find a common ground. Give them compliments and a good reputation to live up to, say, "I know you are a very considerate person, therefore please think about how it makes me feel when you..."

If you feel you gave enough chances but that nothing changed, you can take the next step without remorse. If you back out of the friendship overnight, without any previous warning, you'll leave an unfair situation behind that will make you feel remorse, guilt, and other mentally cluttering negative feelings that are in opposition to mental minimalism.

The best mental minimalism motto in this case is: "treat others as you'd like to be treated." This is such a simple rule to live up to, and it makes your relationships so much smoother. Avoid strangers and acquaintances who bring you down, talk about your problems with your friends, and be grateful and cherish those relationships that make you most happy.

When your attitude is the problem

There's no perfect relationship: be it a friendship,

romance, or relative. And there shouldn't be. Imagine how boring life would be if there were no different opinions. And here's where it gets tricky: there's a difference between genuinely negative, depressing people, and you becoming depressed because you can't accept a differing opinion.

The next time you feel depressed, anxious, or angry after a conversation with someone, be present and ask yourself the following question:

Why do I feel... (anger, sorrow etc.)?

If you notice the emphasis in your answer is on the difference of the opinions rather than on the topic of the conversation, it's time to practice some introspection and acceptance. It means your attitude is the problem, not the relationship itself. I emphasize: your attitude is the problem. You are not the problem. Don't brood or get stuck in an ascetic mood. Just try to change your attitude.

Some people can't accept (constructive) criticism or differing opinions, thus their relationships become very fragile and edgy. It's all good until someone agrees with them, but as soon as an opposing opinion appears, they become defensive, bring out the fighter attitude and turn their conversation into an argument.

Why? Why is it better to argue? Does it make your life easier? Better? Let me tell you something, and I'm not the only one to say this. Dale Carnegie agrees with me too. Ok, just kidding, I agree with him. In his book, *How to Win Friends and Influence People* he says that it is the best if they are avoided. Why? It never makes you a winner.

If you lose, you lost – bad feelings, decreased self-confidence, shame, and useless mental clutter spent on recalling the argument again and again. If you are a verbal Bruce Lee and you happen to win the argument, the losing party will feel the same feelings that you felt when you were the losing party. Therefore, you probably won't move up on his popularity list. You win an argument, but you lose the good will of the other person. It may seem like a fine price to pay, but is it really?

Habit becomes personality, and if you often have verbal showdowns with insignificant people, you'll soon do it with the important ones, and you won't even notice. And if they get angry with you, and start considering you an unpleasant person, that will make your self-esteem lower and bring lots of whys and frustrations into your life. Then your thoughts will become cluttered again.

So what's to be done? Don't argue but ask. Someone has a different opinion than you? Wouldn't it be exciting to know why? Instead of attacking the person with your rock-solid opinion, rather, ask why they think what they think.

There's a high likelihood this person will ask about your viewpoint too. That's called a conversation. After the conversation, both of you will go home happy and satisfied knowing that someone showed curiosity in you.

Leaving the fighter attitude out of conversations can save you lots of nerves and can keep people around you.

Romantic Relationships

In my opinion, you can practice minimalism in your relationships by reducing expectations as much as possible. Reduce expectations about how you expect yourself to behave in the relationship, and also how you expect your partner to behave.

Managing your relationship expectations will free you from getting caught up in disappointment, frustration, and distress. This rule applies to all your relationships, not just your romantic ones. But, I have the feeling that most expectations are linked to romantic affairs.

When I was a kid, ok even in my early twenties, I had a 10-point list of things I expected to find in the perfect guy. These points included such serious demands as being a cat lover, and wearing a uniform. I know I've disappointed you now, but for the record, I've kicked eight points off my list since then, including the aforementioned two. I've kept only two, which hold the essence of a romantic affair:

1. My ideal partner is someone with whom I can be myself and who loves me for who I am.
2. My ideal partner is someone I can fully accept and love for who he is, without wanting to change him.

I really think these two simple statements provide

a stable foundation for any relationship. Everything else is fairy dust, something we think is important but in reality doesn't matter.

Our relationships are supposed to lift us up, help us grow, and make us better people. They should be our home where we feel that we're in a judgment and expectation-free area. This doesn't mean life will be like in LaLa Land. There will be misunderstandings and differences of opinions. That's normal. As long as we're willing to accept that our partner is a human being, an individual with different thoughts than us, arguments will be a short and constructive. As soon as expectations and demands take over reason, our romantic relationship will turn into the most complicated, annoying source of mental clutter ever.

It is more important to ask, listen, and accept your partner's differing opinion than it is others – you share most of your time with your partner, after all. It is good to know a lot about how he or she thinks and how you two can you appreciate your differing thoughts. Be present, listen carefully, and don't approach disagreements with negativity even if this sounds weird in the beginning.

If you constantly repress your partner's opinion or argue heavily with it, he or she will be less inclined to tell you things. Then you'll start wondering (cluttering your mind with tangling thoughts) why your partner is distant and unwilling to talk. If you don't practice enough self-criticism, you'll end up with explanations like: he's cheating, or she doesn't love me anymore.

Always do some honest introspection first. Don't jump into finding external explanations before you've made sure there's no internal reason.

Think about your behavior with your partner. Then ask yourself this question: would you like to switch places with your partner? Would you like to be in a relationship with yourself? Would you accept yourself?

If your answer to these questions is an honest "yes," then it means you're on the right track. If, however, you wouldn't like to have yourself as a partner, it's time to start some self-evaluation.

Why wouldn't you like to be in a relationship with yourself?

Why can't you accept yourself?

Why do you think you can accept your partner if you can't accept yourself?

These are tough questions but worth considering. In most cases, we complicate our love life because we're not ok with ourselves. We push our own fears on our partner. If we were cheated on before, let's say, we're constantly jealous when other women or men are around our significant other. Of course, this is only the case if we can't leave our past behind.

Comparison is a dangerous tool. If you compare your current relationship to one that ended badly in the past, you can easily bring the past into the present without meaning to. It will mess up your peace of mind, that's for sure.

And in stepping into the realm of mental minimalism, we not only have to let go of objects, but also of bad memories, unhealthy comparisons, and unfair expectations. Let me share a simple example.

Just imagine you hold a huge ball in your hands (one like those big rubber balls in gyms that people only seem to sit on). That ball is your past. There is, however, another ball nearby – a nicer one with ribbons and filled with candies – it is the future ball. And you desperately want it, but your hands are busy with this other ball, from your past. It doesn't matter how much you struggle, when your hands are full with one big ball, you can't pick up the other.

What can you do? You can't grow two more hands. You have to put down the past ball, let go of it, and empty your hands. When your hands are free again, then you can pick up the future ball. There is no room for the both.

The same applies to your mind. As long as your mind is busy with the past, it can't focus on building a better future. Each relationship deserves a clean sheet – do a mental declutter before each new relationship. Do not let your past poison your present and doom your future.

I can summarize this chapter in three takeaway

sentences:

-    Give people a chance to correct their behavior. If they don't, consider your needs first.
-    Don't argue, listen.
-    Leave expectations and comparisons behind, and let go of the past.

Chapter 5: The Simple Life Overall

I was wondering if I should start the book with this chapter, but I feared it would steal the show from the other chapters, with its less conventional meaning of minimalism. We've explored minimalism as a mindset, but how can this mindset improve our environment, our inner peace, and our relationships with others.

By the time you rewire your brain in these three areas according to your new minimalist worldview and you re-arrange your home, your soul, and your social connections, you'll want more. You'll want to stick to this mindset and live your life accordingly. Not because I say to, or because you need to, but because you'll feel happier and like life is easier doing so.

"Minimalism is a tool that can assist you in finding freedom. Freedom from fear. Freedom from worry. Freedom from being overwhelmed. Freedom from guilt. Freedom from depression. Freedom from the trappings of the consumer culture we've built our lives around. Real freedom." This is Joshua Fields Millburn and Ryan Nicodemus's definition from their successful site theminimalist.com. I couldn't agree more.

Minimalism is the liberating feeling that comes from living a carefree life. It's the best tool we can use to pursue happiness. The focus is not on the name itself. In my opinion, it is just called minimalism because people can organize and relate their thoughts and actions better around something that has a tale-tell name, like the word minimalism does. In practice, it's not something with lots of theoretical explanations, but rather, individual desires taken to the level of action.

Let me illustrate this through two stories of how others achieved their minimalist lifestyles. These include everything we've talked about up to now (environmental, mental, social minimalism) and much more.

Cait's consumerism combat

Cait Flanders started blogging in a time of hardship. She had a large amount of debt to pay off, and so she created the blog to share her journey with people in similar circumstances. In 2013 she finally met her goal of becoming debt-free. When she turned 29, instead of doing reckless things she'd regret the next morning that certain pop hits encourage people to do, she decided to embrace her own understanding of minimalism with a one-year shopping ban. She gave away 75 percent of her stuff and reduced her spending to only what was necessary.

Why? Cait shares many reasons for her shopping ban in her blog post. In one of them she writes, "I finally acknowledged that I'd let lifestyle inflation creep in after becoming debt-free, and realized nothing I'd been spending money on was bringing me joy." Today, she is a fierce revolutionary fighting consumerism. She realized how wretched it could turn one's life, without providing any happiness.

In her perception, a minimalist lifestyle is one in which people don't waste their money on things. Where a low-waste and debt-free life buys happiness; where you can't buy happiness by buying stuff.

Just think about your most recent shopping spree. The time you felt that you MUST buy something, or your life wouldn't feel complete. This can apply to anything: food, alcohol, clothing, household equipment, etc. Did you feel this rush for possessions because you needed that red jacket or because another part of your life was lacking? Was it easier to fill your life with something else rather than deal with the real problem.

Let me confess something to you. When I lived alone, from the age of fourteen to twenty, I spent most my money on clothes. I did. I had so many clothes. Sometimes I spent 85 percent of my monthly budget on just one pair of trousers. Why? Because I wanted to be accepted by my classmates. Today, it seems crazy, even to me, that I did that, but back then, being alone, far away from anybody who cared about me, I desperately wanted to be loved by those who surrounded me.

I was at a pricey private school, one of only a few

kids there on a scholarship. Most of the kids were in a much better financial situation. And this was reflected in their clothes. Thanks to the consumerist demands of the 21st century, and the small-town effect, they'd also all known each other since long before high school. They had a collective mindset that everyone who was not of their status, was an outsider. In my 14-year-old brain, I figured that if I started to resemble them, somehow I'd gain access to their circle. The emphasis was not on them being rich, like being rich was a bad thing, the emphasis (to me) was on achieving an unreachable level of consumerism upon which they formed their judgment.

I started working, saving money, finding alternative sources of food just to meet their standards and not die of hunger in the meantime. Long story short, I spent all my money; I accumulated a cartload of stuff, but failed to achieve acceptance or happiness. What I got in return was a constant fear of not being able to make ends meet. I wondered how I would make enough to buy my next must-have item... It was a dark and vicious cycle.

For one reason or another, many of you are in the same shoes as I was. Buying things to compensate for a lack of love, upgrading smartphones to compensate for a lack of coolness, buying the newest makeup and trendiest clothing to compensate for a lack of confidence... Don't tell me. Just look deeply into your soul. Did any of these things bring you the results you wanted? Did the new smartphone, which I don't want to be a commercial for but, you know, the logo looks like a popular fruit, make you more popular?

Did it maybe attract a few curious colleagues who envied it for five minutes before moving on, resenting you for getting it sooner than they did. Now you've got their attention, but they don't have yours. But at the end of the day, their interest was not in you, but in your phone. And they don't like you better. So what's the purpose of filling your life with useless items to impress people?

Look for the real reason. Why do you overeat? Why do you overspend? There's always a reason for excess.

Minimalism is the tool for finding your freedom. When it comes to consumption, minimalism can be found in your answer to this question:

What am I compensating for with this?

In a podcast with Tim Ferriss, Derek Sivers, my all-time favorite contemporary thinker, once said, that there should be parrots in every supermarket to fly above people's heads and say, "it won't make you happy." Such a funny idea, but a legit message, if you think about it.

If you have the opportunity, by all means, get such a parrot and take it with you each time you go shopping. But, if for some reason you can't get the bird, create a parrot in your head that whenever you go shopping repeats in a silly parrot voice: *it won't make you happy.*

Think about a time when you successfully overcame the urge to spend recklessly, take a step back and examine why you felt you needed that Milanese or shoe, or whatnot. This process belongs to the mental decluttering category.

As I mentioned there, you'll need three things: acceptance, introspection, and selfishness.

You need to accept that you don't really need that thing, even if it feels like you do. Use introspection to detect the reason that lies behind your urge.

And when you've got the answer, be selfish enough to choose yourself instead of the perceived or real reasons of please others with your purchase.

These reasons can be numerous, and letting go of them and stepping onto the path of minimalism might not be easy. It wasn't for me.

It took more than five years after I left the upper east side of this small town to leave behind my obsessive compulsion to shop for branded clothes. I needed to go through all the steps of mental decluttering. First, I had to admit and accept that yes, I wasted a lot of money hoping for a different result. Then, through introspection, I found what I was actually looking for: I wanted to be accepted, loved, and to belong in that circle.

I realized I put the acceptance expectations on the wrong side on the equation. First, I had to accept myself, then seek acceptance. But I couldn't accept myself yet because I believed I wasn't good enough because I didn't have enough money. The world is a mirror, what you see is what you get.

There is an old story from the ancient Greece. Socrates and his pupil stood at the gates of Athens and talked about philosophy. A wayfarer crossed their path and asked Socrates:

-    Oh, wise Socrates. I came from a far away land and I'm worried about entering the city. I believe that in Athens people are genuinely unpleasant and disgraceful. Is that true?
-    I'm afraid so. You'll meet lots of people like that here.

The wayfarer went on despondently. A few minutes later, another wayfarer arrived at the city gates:

-      Oh, wise Socrates. I came from a faraway land, and I'm so happy to be here. I believe that in Athens people are genuinely kind and welcoming. Is that true?

-      I believe so. You'll meet lots of people like that here.

The second wayfarer happily entered the city. The pupil looked puzzled and asked his master:

-      Master Socrates, why did you lie to one of these people?

-      I didn't lie. What you truly believe is what you'll get.

And how simple and truthful this little anecdote is. I'd like to add that the root of negative expectations of others is rooted in a person's own negative self-evaluation. Even when it seems it's not about you, it still is. In my case, I was an outsider because I believed I was one and I acted like one. I thought it was not my fault, but partially it was.

The real breakthrough, however, came when I gave away almost all my clothes after my experience with the cherry trees that I mentioned in the beginning of this book. Minimalism truly set me free. Not only from the excess of my possessions, but also from my buried scars and pains. And, as I let all it go, an inexplicable calmness ran through me.

The other inspiring story I read about living by minimalist standards is somewhat different than Cait's, although she does eagerly do the same activity as the couple I'm about to introduce. This couple gave away, literally, everything in their late 30s. Why? Let me tell you.

Traveling with the Talbots

I came across Warren and Betsy's story by chance when I was downloading podcasts before a transatlantic plane journey. This sweet American couple who is "married with their luggage," have been on the road for years. They seemed tireless and full of energy on their podcast. Let's see what minimalism is from their, and more generally speaking, a world traveller's view.

The Talbots' impulse to make a minimalist life-change wasn't mental clutter, not even a physical one – even though they'd both been married before so they both brought their fully equipped household to their relationship. The reason the Talbots jumped into the bohemian, minimal lifestyle of backpacking was the realization of the mortality of the human body. Betsy's brother had a heart attack in his 30s, and another friend around the same age had a brain aneurysm.

Being thirty-seven themselves, Betsy and Warren agreed: their life must be lived, no regrets, no excuses. They asked themselves this question:

"How would we change our lives if we knew we wouldn't make it to our 40th birthdays?"

The commitment to make the change was fixed. They knew their "whys" so the only thing missing was the answer to the question of what they would do now? One casual afternoon, they started talking about what they should do, and soon they agreed. They wanted to see the world. So, in the following few hours they outlined their saving plans and started to make preparations for a year of travel. This was in 2008. Since 2010 they've been on the road. They are happy and living a life they always wanted.

In the podcast, Warren said that a year was never

enough, but that the first thing you had to do was: "open your mind to the concept of a year." The first step is difficult; rewiring your brain is not easy. Opening up to a minimalist lifestyle can be just as scary as it is exciting. But when you decide to engage in the process, and you can see that you actually can live with less, "It's empowering."

It makes you wonder what world travelers who have it all miss the most? Warren and Betsy said they miss nothing but the experiences with their friends and family.

Happiness can't be bought with money. And as we learned from the movie *Into the Wild*, "happiness is only real if shared." Warren and Betsy have each other, but they truly miss sharing their thoughts and excitement with their loved ones.

They don't miss their house, their TV, or their belongings. People hardly ever do. (Except when you travel deep in Eastern Europe. Then I find you really start missing your toilet at home.)

I grew up in my grandparent's house. I lived with them until I was six. If I'm ever asked where I truly feel at home, I think of that little village house. When they died, and my parents wanted to sell the house, I protested. That was my home!! It was the only place in the entire world I felt safe and like I belonged. How could they think about selling it?

But I was just a kid and there was nothing I could do. They took me down to collect the things I wanted from the house. It was the first (and last) time I entered the house without my grandparents being there. And, let me tell you, it was empty. The furniture was unchanged. My grandpa's half-broken, glued-together eyeglasses were still on top of his small radio. One of his bottles of tomato juice still had a few sips left. My grandmother's knitting kit was on the table. The last dishes they'd used were on the drying rack... Nothing changed. But everything changed.

But the soul was not there anymore. The house was empty. Objects are meaningless by themselves. It's always because of the people when we get attached to something. But without the people, they lose their meaning.

In 2017 it will be ten years since my grandparents passed away. I loved them as if they'd been my parents. However, I've never carried a gadget of theirs with me. I don't need any object to remember them. I've only kept my grandfather's broken eyeglasses and a toy I gave to my grandmother, which she slept with after I moved to my parents. I keep these relics in my drawer. Nothing more.

Memories don't need tools. You need a simple,

open heart to remember. Some people wish for their names to be remembered or feared or cherished even after they are gone. I think everybody lives until there's a place for them in someone else's heart.

It doesn't matter if you wish for your life to be a travel movie or a more stationary one, the only things you will truly miss are the things that are irreplaceable. Every object can be replaced. This is what I've learned from listening to the Talbot's story, and what I've also learned for myself.

If we learn to care less about objects and more about those who are dearest to us, our quality of life will increase and become more simple. Human relationships can be quite twisted and even painful from time to time, but they also bring us the most joy. And, if we handle them with the right attitude, even the nuisances seem like a piece of cake to endure.

The best example for this is Christmas Eve. Imagine a situation in which there are no presents, but you can be around every person you love. Close your eyes and try to recall that heartwarming feeling that comes when you gather around the tree, look at each other and say Merry Christmas, and hold each person in a warm embrace. No gifts, just pure love.

Now imagine a cartload of gifts under your tree, but that you are standing alone. Everyone you care about is dead or didn't want to spend Christmas Eve with you. Just in reading these lines and picturing the situation how do you feel?

Most of us feel pain and a sense of deep solitude. Objects can grant comfort, even an insincere popularity, but nothing replaces your mother's warm smile or your child's honest laughter.

That's why I prefer gifting my loved ones experiences instead of objects. I know that going together to do something fun or exciting or making a connection will have a much deeper and longer-term value than buying more clutter.

Sometimes gifting experiences seems overpriced, but the concept itself is highly underrated. Some people think, *why should I spent x money on those two hours of performance when I can buy this boot for the same amount of money and it lasts ten years?* Because the activity itself might last only 2 hours, but the enjoyment of experience lasts forever.

I've written down many definitions of minimalism constructed by others. Here's mine that I composed after that one month of physical, mental, social, and lifestyle de-cluttering.

Minimalism, to me, is a process where you

maximize your happiness by sticking to minor changes. Let go instead of collecting – be it objects or past grievances – accept instead of revolt, and commit instead of expect.

The key minimalism takeaways from this chapter are:

-      Spend less on objects, value experiences instead.

-      When you own almost nothing, what you'll miss the most are things that can't be bought.

Chapter 6: The Twelve Months of a New Year

Hey, all ya minimalists! Since it's almost New Years, I invite you to participate in a challenge. I promised I'd help you stick to a minimalist lifestyle even after you got on track with what you sought from this book.

Minimalism, in my opinion, can't be restricted to decluttering, or maintaining only well-working relationships, but all and everything that's human. We talked about how minimalism is a privilege, and how much freedom it gives a person. Ultimately, it's a tool that brings you maximum joy with minimal effort and few negative by-products.

Minimalism is also about simplicity. Simplifying our lives shouldn't involve complicated exercises and practices because it would go against the main concept.

Obtaining minimalism in different life areas involves simple practices. I talked about them in the previous chapters. Maintaining minimalism is similar.

And here comes the minimalist challenge. The rules are simple: you must practice one act of minimalism each day. I outline four life areas where you should practice these short exercises. Each life area will need three months practice time. And four multiplied by three is twelve – one year.

The exercises will assume that you've already made the commitment to simplify all the areas of your life that are mentioned in this book. I'd like you to keep a journal about your minimalist project. I encourage you to buy one thing only for it: a pocket calendar. But if you are more of an online organizer, just put what I'll ask in the following pages in in your computer's calendar. Just make sure to not forget about it.

1.   The First Quarter

So the first life area is physical decluttering. I started the book with this chapter, and I will ask you to start your year with it. (I will start by using the month of January, but if you buy my book in April, let's say, start with April.)

January: Get rid of something each day. Even if you completed a big decluttering project recently, I'm pretty sure there are some survivors that could go. If there's really nothing left you want to throw away, just wait one or two days: a newspaper, a new shoe, your 2016 calendar... Something will get outdated.

You can also be resourceful and throw away something virtual, like old information or unnecessary screenshots or files from your computer. But, use the online de-cluttering only when you really don't have anything physical to throw away.

Write down on your calendar what you threw away each day. Just a short definition such as *expired sour cream, yesterday's newspaper, empty toothpaste*, etc.

February: Now it's time for you to get a bit more organized. Look around your home, your office desk, and if something doesn't have a place, find a place for it. If something is weirdly placed, find a better place for it.

Keep track of your progress in your journal. Again, just give a short description of your daily action: *put photo frame on the top of the TV, milk to the fridge's door instead of the shelf, putting plates on lower shelf where I can reach them better.*

... It can be anything. The point is to make your home more transparent and livable.

March: Fix, replace, and improve. The last month of this 3-month block is about improving every useful item that is in its rightful place now.

Keep track of each change in your journal: *change the light bulb in the shower, buy a working coffee machine, use two pillows for better sleep...*

2.   The Second Quarter

This three-month block will help you improve your inner stability.

April: Get motivated. It's spring, new life, cherry trees and all, so time for some positive vibes for the brain. Each day, read a positive quote and put it on your calendar. Do not spend more than a minute searching for it. Put a topic in Google like *daily confidence* or *courage* and pick the first option on the results page. Think about the message of the quote.

May: It's getting pleasantly warm outside (sorry friends in Alaska). This month's challenge is to eat or drink one of your daily meals outside in nature. It can be a full meal or just a snack. In the meantime, meditate. Let your thoughts flow freely.

Write what you ate on your calendar. Where did you eat it? What were you thinking about during that time?

June: Time to catch those negative mind monkeys.

Since it's summer and the sun is shining, it's a good time to visit the shady areas of your soul. Each day, keep track of your main negative thoughts (self-judgment, fears...). And write their opposite in your journal. For example, if you thought you weren't good enough, write in your journal that you ARE good enough. Repeat that a few times, and try to believe it.

If you do that with maximum commitment, after a time when you start thinking about something negative, you'll automatically start to think about it's positive counterpart so you can put that into your journal. At the end of the day, the positive thought will be the last one you have.

3.   The Third Quarter

Now you probably expect me to say relationship declutter. Haha, wrong. The next three months will be about your health. The exercises will be very simple and the only thing you'll have to write in your journal is a check mark when you're done. (I didn't use the word "if" intentionally.)

July: Eat five vegetables each day. They are healthy, contain lots of vitamins and are very low in calories so you can easily maintain that summer beach body by following this advice.

August: Drink at least two liters (more than half a gallon) of water each day. It's summer, it's hot outside, and your body needs more hydration.

September: Go for at least a 30-minute walk each day. If you do another type of exercise, do the walking in addition to it. It's about minimal habit consistency, not only the physical motion.

4.   The Fourth Quarter

The last three months will help you see and

appreciate the values and good qualities of other people.

October: This month, try to find some good in your partner. If you are single, then in somebody close to you. Focus on the good in the people closest to you. Write your observations in your journal: *today she helped an old lady catch the bus, today he smiled at me lovingly, today she helped me with my accounting...* See the good in people you love even more.

As a bonus exercise, at the end of the month show your significant other or friend how many special qualities they have that they might not even have noticed.

November: Do good. Last month you paid attention and appreciated the bright side of others. This month, be the bright side. Do something small for your partner or a friend to make them happy – wash the dishes, bring them a small chocolate, or tell them a silly joke or a compliment. Write your acts of kindness in your journal and feel how uplifting it is to make someone else happy.

December: Take a judgment-free month. We encounter minor or major annoyances each day and feel pissed by them. Sometimes we even take them personally. This month, each day, when something upsets you with something, remind yourself that everyone is doing the best that they can. And nothing they do is personal. Try to understand their perspective and think about what you would you do in their place.

Write your achievements in this department in your journal: *today my husband forgot the fridge's door opened, but I resisted the temptation to get annoyed with him, today my co-worker spoke too loudly on the phone, but I resisted the urge to tell her to stop since she doesn't do it often, today the sales lady miscalculated my bill, but I let it go with a kind warning, I know she didn't do it on purpose...* Understand, forgive, and love. This is what December is all about, isn't it?

The point of the routine this minimalist year is to improve and get better each day. Take care of your surroundings, your mental and physical health, and your relationships. See that the world is a wonderful, simple place, and that your attitude complicates it. As Captain Jack Sparrow says in *Pirates of the Caribbean*, "The problem is not the problem; the problem is your attitude about the problem."

You're not in a competition with anyone here. Living a simpler and happier life is only about you. My final thought comes from Cait Flanders.

"Be a little bit better of a person than yesterday,

and isn't that the only person you should try to be?"

I believe in you.

Yours truly,

Zoe

P.S.: If you have questions please don't hesitate to contact me on zoemckey@gmail.com. I welcome any kind of constructive opinion as well. I'd like to know how I can help so please share your ideas with me. If you'd like to get helpful tips from me on a weekly basis, visit me at www.zoemckey.com and subscribe. Thank you!

More Books By Zoe

Unbreakable Confidence

Build Grit

Build Social Confidence

Find What You Were Born For – Book 1

Find What You Were Born For – Book 2

Find Who You Were Born To Be

Catching Courage

Fearless

Daily Routine Makeover

Daily Routine Makeover – Morning Edition

Emotional Confidence

Communication and Confidence Coaching

By working with me you can expect to gain a better understanding of yourself, and the hope you need to change your life for the better. I will help you understand everybody around you better starting with yourself. My three main goals are to help you:

- Embrace discomfort to break down your negative beliefs,
- Find your strengths and focus on them,
- Bring out the side of you that is totally comfortable with yourself and your environment.

I have a unique approach to coaching. The entire lesson is composed of two parts:

Interpersonal Skills Development

Do your palms sweat and your heart pound when you enter in a room full of strangers? Do you feel awkward when somebody starts a conversation with you? Do you fear you'll run out of things to say and wish you could just talk casually with everybody?

Then this course was made for you!

In this section, I'll help you learn how to communicate with others, how to be presentable, and how to always make a great impression. Humans are social beings and since you live among them you can never underestimate the importance of social skills. If you have them you can be 100-percent present and aware in any situation. I have been studying and developing communication and real-life social interaction skills for more than 10 years. I've written 10 books – all of them Amazon best-sellers – on the topic. I can help you, please let me!

Here you will learn:

- How to start conversations and keep them going with anybody,
- How to "win friends and influence people,"
- Airy, pleasant ways to be more charming and likable,
- How to be the life of the party, and
- Tips on how to handle difficult conversations and people.

I'll teach you how to be the person everyone notices when you enter the room, the person who instantly sparks people's interest and can talk easily to anyone.

Intrapersonal Skills Development

Is the mirror your worst enemy? Or the scale? Or both? Do you feel uncomfortable with who you are? Do you sometimes feel your days are passing by without any purpose? Is sleeping your favorite activity? Do you wish you were somewhere else, maybe someone else?

If any of these statements apply to you then you have work to do. Living with self-contempt, regrets, and frustration is not sustainable. In this part of the coaching I will help you to accept and recover from any inner struggles you have. With honesty and commitment, I will guide you to let go of old wounds, and help you find your strengths and develop them in order to bring out the best in yourself.

I'll help you:

- to discover the root cause of your problems,
- recover from childhood traumas,
- communicate with yourself objectively and silence the malicious voices in your head,
- build confidence and self-respect, and learn to be persistent and get what you want.

If you're interested, apply here:

http://www.zoemckey.com/contact/